How to Stand Up to Bullying

M. C. Ryder

They are the
thunder

You are the

lightning

MC
ryder

M.E.C. Publishing— Lebanon County, PA
ISBN: 979-8-9885074-0-6
eBook ISBN: 979-8-9885074-1-3
Library of Congress Control Number: 2023912200
Title: *How to Stand Up to Bullying*
Author: M. C. Ryder
Digital distribution | 2023
Paperback | 2023

Dedication

To my grandma, I am who I am today because of you. Rest in peace. And to my childhood bullies, thank you for challenging me…

Acknowledgements

I would like to first thank a good friend of mine, Becca, for being supportive in my author journey, in coming across a local writer's group, and asking me to join her. It never crossed my mind to search for a writer's group at a local library.

To the writer's group at Lebanon Community Library, thank you for the warm welcome and a safe place where I could read my written words. I was always apprehensive to read my works to an audience, but you all helped me cross that bridge and gain more confidence in myself. For that I am ever grateful.

And lastly, to you the readers. There are so many reasons why I write, but at the end of the day it's always for you. The only way I know how to make a difference in this huge broken world is to write words that can hopefully have an impact in your lives. To let you know you are not alone even when you feel that you are. To inspire and help you stand up for yourself. If there is one thing you should take away, it's that you are good enough as you are. Change for no one but yourself. Do not dwell in your pain. Be the change you wish to see and choose kindness.

Acknowledgments

Table of Contents

Chapter 1
What is a Bully?

Before we begin, we must first define what a bully is. In my experience, a bully is one who repeatedly uses words or actions to beat one down, usually emotionally but sometimes physically, in order to rise above. Treats with disrespect. Intimidates in order to get what he/she wants, whatever that may be. Constantly harasses in a habitual manner.

If something is habitual, it's either habit or intentional. If it's habit, it's automatic. If it's intentional, it's deliberate. The same goes for one who bullies. A bully either doesn't realize they are being cruel or they enjoy inflicting pain. There are always two sides to view everything. The crucial factor both have in common is how *you* utilize *your* voice. If you say nothing, they think the action is okay. If you do use your voice, they will be quick to get offended and try to silence you for calling them out on it.

Let's take a deeper dive. A bully is basically a repeated offender. Unwarranted persistent behavior that escalates over time until it becomes out of control.

I recall from my childhood a lie I was told, that's probably still told today, that the other kid(s) who tease and make fun may secretly like you. That is a toxic mentality to have as a young child and gives an excuse that makes the unwanted behavior okay. That behavior is *never* okay. That's the behavior that needs corrected, immediately. Of course, the child is going to throw a tantrum when they are told to stop. It's because they are not getting what they want and are getting called out on the thing that gives them attention. In a sense, it's a cry for help. They don't know how to communicate what it is they want and find it in a negative way. The longer they get the attention they want, in a negative way, the more it becomes habitual until they can't see that it's the wrong way to get what they want. Never reward bad behavior. If you do, it just teaches them to take what they want by force.

Let's dive darker.

Everything begins at a young age. There's a wise quote by Alice Miller, "Nobody is born evil." That is absolutely true. It's learned. There's another quote that speaks volumes by Nelson Mandela, "No one is born hating another person because of the color of his skin, or his background, or his religion. People must learn hate, and if they can learn to hate, they can be taught to love, for love comes more naturally to the human heart than its opposite."

Bullying is a form of hate. When a child feels unwanted or unloved, they grow to resent love and turn to hate. The same is true for all of us, every day. When you are constantly misunderstood, ignored, or forced to be someone other than yourself, you turn to hate. What we all want is to be seen, to be heard, and to be loved. The same goes for a child. What the child does not understand is why their parents are never around, when the parents have to work to keep a roof over their head and food on the table. What the child does not understand is why their parents always yell when they are around, when the parents are tired and stressed. All children know is they are being neglected. They are too young to comprehend their emotions and lash out in a negative way. That's the only time they get attention, even if it's the wrong kind of attention. That learned behavior gets transferred to school. A repeated cycle in which the system generally fails them. That toxic behavior gets redirected to the innocent.

Evil and hate is not congenital. Neither is bullying. It's always a choice, but when one walks down the wrong path with no guidance it's hard to unlearn a bad habit. Not impossible, but it's difficult to undo the damage done. That child eventually becomes an adult who may eventually have a child of their own where the cycle continues to be repeated. It's hard for someone to open themselves to love when they never learned what true love was to begin with. All they learned from early on was heartache and vulnerability that broke them repeatedly. Hard to love someone when you never learned how to love yourself first.

There are hidden dangers when the bullying behavior does not get corrected early on. As a child, they don't understand their actions are hurting others. They are redirecting their pain onto someone else without realizing it. They find they have control of the environment they may not have control of elsewhere. As more time slides by, that dominating influence turns to manipulating. They have control of the puppet strings. Advantage of one's emotions. Becomes an addiction of self-interest. The more influence they gain over others, eventually it turns to narcissism. Now the situation has become dire. Once that level is reached, it's very hard to retrain the mind. Not impossible, but that mind has closed around taking advantage of others. No one wanted to see them, hear them, love them. When an open mind closes, it's strenuous for one to find that key as it would mean opening themselves back up to vulnerability.

Chapter 2
Psychology of a Bully

Intentional or not intentional, when someone habitually uses intimidation to get what they want, that is bullying. Everyone gets bullied, *every day*. A lot of times, you don't even realize it. On the road, a tailgater is pushing you to go faster. A honking of the horn in stop and go traffic does nothing other than to aggravate with harassment. Even ads you hear or see on television prey on you persistently for you to get something you don't necessarily need.

In my debut, *The Darkest Side of the Moon*, there's a scene where Nadine reflects back to her childhood to the first time she ever stood up to a bully. That was not fiction. That was me. I was that little girl. I stood up to a bully when he took a soccer ball from another girl during recess. That was a defining moment in my life when the "power" shifted into my own hands. I was no longer under the bully's influence. I gained confidence that day. Confidence not to allow myself to be knocked down anymore. To question intent. The confidence is in *all* of us.

Break the cycle of thinking. It's *not* okay for someone to treat you like you are not good enough. You have nothing to prove to *anyone* your worth. Just know what you bring to the table. If they don't want to provide mutual respect, then leave. You are better off anyway. You never have to settle for something less than your worth. There are those out there that will respect what you have to offer, you just have to find the right individuals. Keep those who see something in you around before you make a name for yourself and remember those who were eager to turn their backs on you. There's a reason. There's always a reason why something didn't work out the way you wanted it to. It wasn't meant to be because you were meant for something better. When they realize they missed out on an opportunity, they will be begging. Don't ever let them in. Their intentions are not pure. You gave them one chance; they don't deserve another. Listen and grasp that saying by Anthony Weldon, "Fool me once shame on you; Fool me twice shame on me."

Bullies, predators, always prey on the weak. Why? Because it boosts their ego. It's the easiest way for them to get what they want, even if they don't know what it is. Everyone, including myself, is quick to cast them off due to the toxic, negative behavior, but why are they acting out in the manner in the first place? What molded them into thinking they can use negative behavior to get what they want? Because someone failed them in life. A parent, a teacher, a friend, or even a coworker. Or all of the above.

Growing up I had multiple bullies in my life, but there is one that stands out. One that treated me so cruel I associated two things whenever I was in the same room as him; fear and hate. That's right, I learned to hate. Hated the way he made me feel. Wanted nothing to do with him and went out of my way to avoid him at all costs. He knew the right words to say to trigger me. He was toxic, but I kept my mouth shut and took the beatings of razor-sharp words.

One day I found myself at lunch with his tough as nails girlfriend. Not typically someone I associated myself with, but she didn't treat me like he did. She had her own personal problems and she shared a bit about his family problems. Particularity with his father. In that moment, I stopped seeing him as a monster and was able to empathize. I could now associate where the toxic behavior came from. Doesn't make what he did to me and the others right, it was just his way of lashing out without getting a beating at home. At home he didn't have a voice. At school he ran his mouth. He didn't have the same fear at school as he did at home. He was the driving force in my character Greg in *The Darkest Side of the Moon.*

There was another incident during my time at school that's important to share. I had another bully that even teachers feared. He was a transfer and didn't last long, but he left a lasting memory that I still think about from time to time. I remember the day clearly. How I stood up to him and how he threatened to spray me in the eyes with a chemical. I took the reins after the teacher had instructed him to settle down as he was being loud and opinionated, which encouraged his followers to be loud and opinionated. They didn't listen. I grew frustrated. When I opened my mouth and called him out on it, he didn't like that. To be honest, he was a worse monster than my childhood bully. Looked and acted like he belonged to a gang. When he threatened to spray me in the face with a chemical, I reported it to the teacher, who even saw it. She failed me that day. She should have had my back, but fear was stronger.

Feared standing up to him. I will admit, I was afraid too, but I learned by then not to let fear hold me back. Walking home, I remained alert. If I feared there was one person who would have brought a weapon to school, it was him. Lucky for me, he was pulled from school shortly after never to be seen or heard of again.

With that in mind, let me ask a very important question. Why are there so many tragedies at schools? Everyone is quick to point the blame to guns. They don't pull their own triggers. They are inanimate objects. When a person hits rock bottom, that's when tragedies occur. A person can only endure for so long until they snap. It should *never* be easy for anyone to take another life without so much as blinking an eye. If one is able to, they have been manipulated.

My first year at a summer job, I met a guy. He was goofy and liked to have fun. Our job required uniforms. He also required a uniform at the school he attended. One day he came to work with pink shoe laces. It became a big deal for him. Was told he had to remove them, but he didn't want to. It was the one thing that allowed him to express himself. Unfortunately, at the job, it was against the dress code policy. I saw both sides of it. The company wanted everyone to look and act a certain way while my friend just wanted to be able to be free to express himself outside of a controlling environment, his school. He went from one controlling environment to another. He couldn't escape from it. Found a defying way around it. Pink shoe laces. It shouldn't have been a big deal, but it was. Unfortunately, after that event, in our second year together at the job, he down-spiraled and ended up getting fired. I noticed a big difference in him between our first and second year at the job. His light snuffed out. A different kind of tragedy.

I'm not a psychologist. Didn't take any course work on the subject, although it does fascinate me. I'm not an expert with a fancy degree, but I am a victim of bullying. My knowledge stems from my lifelong experiences in school, at work, and at home even. In fact, I will admit, sometimes I'm even guilty of it myself. We all are. When you get a positive reaction, that's meaningful to you, you will do anything to continue to receive that positive energy that boosts your soul until it becomes an addiction. What is the true meaning of life? It's one where you can be full in happiness. Unfortunately, our society chains us. Expectations chain us. There are more hours in the day you are compelled to do what you *don't* want to do. If you want a roof over your head and food on the table, you have to work for a living. If you want to make more money, you need to go to college to earn a degree in order to be taken seriously. You ever stop to think why college students party hard all the time? It's because for the first time in their life, they are unchained from expectations at home and school. For the first time in their eighteen years of life, they can be free to be who they want to be. Some take it too far though.

Let's take a look at stealing. Why do people steal? There is always a reason. Maybe because they are too poor to afford it, it's an experiment, or they were urged to do something wrong in order to fit in with the in crowd. Whatever the reason, right and wrong gets blurred until all that's left is entitlement. The thrill of doing something and getting away with it causes one

9

to lose their compass of morality.

An act of kindness can make a difference and save lives. Why? It provides hope. Provides a light when someone might be drowning in a dark tunnel of despair. If we all claim to want world peace, it starts with kindness. The kind where you expect nothing in return. A warm heart is the best reward. Actions always speak louder than words.

When I was out of town, I stopped at a Dunkin and gave the employee a $5 tip. She acted as if I handed over a million dollars. Even questioned if I was sure I wanted to just hand over $5 to put in the tip mug. It's sad that people don't know how to react when people show some kindness and expect nothing in return. We are all too used to negativity and being berated. Money can't buy happiness, only a dose. The more generous actions you make will become the new norm in time, but it starts with you. If you feel broken and miserable inside, everyone around you does too. They might just disguise it differently. Shower with love. Remember, opposites attract. The same goes for love and hate.

Chapter 3
Why do Bullies Bully?

John Fitzherbert was the first to reference the common phrase we know today as, "you can't teach an old dog new tricks." Wrong. I may not be the *Dog Whisperer* or an expert when it comes to dogs, but you can absolutely teach an old dog new tricks. The first step is, you have to build mutual respect. The same goes for all of us.

Why do bullies bully? They prey on your fears. Put you down in order to lift themselves up. Use the thing you are most scared of against you as incentive to their self-esteem. Your reaction feeds their appetite. It's not about you. It's about them. They are threatened by your indifference because it's outside of their norm. They were raised another way and don't understand. An example, as children we are encouraged to color inside the lines, never outside them. When someone colors outside of the lines, others don't know how to handle it as they go into a whirlwind of disarray. There is nothing wrong with coloring outside of the lines, but it goes against the norm. Against what was taught. As long as there is no harm, color outside of the lines. Never hurts to try something new.

Debates only fuel negative responses. Are quick to derail and lose sight of their purpose. Rather, they become a source of entertainment. They should challenge in a tactful manner to persuade the other side to view an issue in a different light. Remember, there are always two sides to everything. Just because you believe in something doesn't mean you have to go out of your way to make someone else believe in what you believe. Everyone is entitled to their own opinions and decisions. There are always pros and cons. Do not let the noise drown your observations as nonverbal cues reveal everything. Even sniffing excessively is a giveaway.

Let's circle back to respect. Hussein Nishah said, "Respect is earned, not given." When you lose respect for someone, it's hard to gain back. Not impossible, but it will be strenuous. When someone loses my respect, I mentally shut them out. If they try to regain my trust, I question their intentions. Let's think back to the old dog who supposedly can't learn new tricks. You know nothing about the old dog. Where he came from or what was in his past. The only thing you know is he's old. You're already making assumptions. Are quick to give up on him. He senses that and matches your stubbornness. You already think he's unintelligent, so why should he bother showing you otherwise? Why should he give you what you want when you're not giving him what he wants? Respect is also compromise. Meeting halfway in understanding. When you understand where he's coming from, he'll be receptive in complying knowing where you're coming from.

The same goes for children. Parents and adults have a prejudice against children who are young and naïve and still developing. While those are all true, ignorance blinds them. Children and adolescents don't know how to express themselves, so they act out. They try to communicate, but no one listens because they are not taken seriously. Behavior stems from somewhere and only grows in a negative way the more it is ignored. Children are smarter than adults give them credit for. Poke fun even with the phrase "kids say the darndest things." Kids speak truth. Truth we as adults are embarrassed when they speak out loud in front of others. Are taught one thing in the safety of their home, or school, but out in public they are silenced. Need an example? I was a young child who learned about drugs at school and saw a man purchase a packet of cigarettes. I don't recall the memory, but my mom does. Naturally, as a child, I pointed a finger and announced to the whole store that he was buying "drugs." My mom hushed me and said she would explain later. What really is happening is, children are getting mixed signals. Parents and those in teaching roles, are not always practicing what is being preached. Then children are blamed when they become frustrated not knowing how to process contradictions.

Let's head into the classroom. It's filled with a lot of structure. Not only is children's home life filled with a lot of structure, but they also get the same at school, which, in my opinion, is a lot worse. Now they are being told to act a certain way, to be a certain way, to do things a certain way that might go against what they were taught in the first five years. Children are not easily fooled. They experience things differently. They are born free and society chains them to regulations. They don't get a right to voice their opinions. It's always viewed as bad behavior.

Teachers have a big impact in a child's life.

Teachers can make them or break them. The first step is always earning respect. Yes, you read that right, respect. Respect from a child as an individual. Let me repeat that, respect from a child as an *individual.* Respect a child's differences, even if it goes against the norm. Once that respect is earned, that child will want to please and the bad behavior will stop. How do I know this? You may be shaking your head thinking I'm crazy. Well, let me tell you, I was one of those children. I acted out. I had teachers calling to report my bad behavior, on a daily basis. They couldn't handle me. Why? I didn't know it at the time, but as I reflected back it was because I didn't respect them. Those few teachers that considered me unruly, I experienced negative vibes from. I still remember to this day my favorite Chapstick confiscated and never returned. Don't remember why it was taken from me or the flavor. I just remember it was the teacher's way of overpowering me and taking something that I valued away from me.

When I moved on from the few teachers that I wasn't fond of, I blossomed into a well-mannered little girl who enjoyed learning because I had the right teachers that took the extra time to appreciate me as an individual. Rewarded me for just being me. An example, one day during recess when we were kept inside due to it raining outside, I was that little girl alphabetizing the books on the bookshelf to keep myself occupied and away from the drama. Later on, I got pulled aside by my teacher and the Principle who issued I believe a certificate. I don't remember exactly what I was rewarded with, I just remember that I was terrified at first and then shocked I was noticed by my teacher and the Principle himself. The Principle! To a child, it was like the President of the United States taking note. To a child, being recognized that you did something right is a big deal when all children are used to negative when interacting with a Principle.

The act by my teacher spoke volume to me as a child. So, when I did something wrong, like taking another classmate's piece of gum due to anger, I was consumed with guilt in disappointing my teacher. The worst feeling in the world is letting someone down I respected. Something no one had to tell me not to do again.

The same is true for everyone. When someone lets you down, it cuts deep. Respect and trust go hand in hand. When it's lost, it stings. When it's suppressed, it festers. Funnels into that bad behavior.

Chapter 4
What do Bullies Want?

What do bullies want? To be seen. To be heard. To be loved. At the end of the day, that is what we all want. To be loved for who we are and understood. Appreciated and not taken for granted. It all stems from childhood. There are two paths a child can walk. The right side or the wrong side. When they don't get what they want, they start taking it by force. Too long walking down that dark path cancels every righteous thing they learned and it normalizes the power hunger. Will act out when they are challenged.

Let's redirect our attention to the workplace. Most are a toxic place. I have yet to work at one that isn't. Why are teenagers so eager to leave school behind? They have the hope that "real life" is different until they find out otherwise. The workplace is basically the same environment as school. Go into it with high hopes and expectations only to be squished like a bug. Structured nearly the same. You have the cool kids and you have the outcasts. The only difference is money is involved this time. Now it's a competition who can climb the ladder and make more money to spend more and show off. A toxic mindset.

The ones who do climb the ladder forget where they

came from. Some even go to whatever means in order to rise up. May punish everyone in order to prove a point to one individual so as not to point a finger. The cycle continues to be repeated. Now they are money hungry as well as power hungry.

Power.

What every bully becomes addicted to. Virtues get swept under the rug. The more one does something and gets away with it, the more it becomes normal. A habit. A bad one. They become blinded in what they truly want as they no longer believe they need it. They found a different outlet. Pain. Now pain is what they want. They were in pain and no one supported them. It's hard for someone, especially a child, to reach out and ask for help. It's detrimental when they do and it's not taken seriously. What they end up learning is it's a weakness. They take that moment of weakness and weaponize it. Love is the worst weapon used as manipulation.

Yehuda Berg stated, along with some others, "Hurt people, hurt people." A bully is someone who has been hurt. Unfortunately, they take it to the extreme. So much so that they turn to manipulation and narcissism. They no longer want love. They fear it actually. Will run away from it. Believe they are undeserving. Now they feed on hate. Bringing one down, raises them up. They use words that cut like a knife. Will continue to stab you with hurtful words and relish in releasing their pain onto you.

Take a moment to think about some of the greatest villains from a movie, television show, or even a book. Several come to my mind. What do they want? World domination? Why? What do they want to dominate?

Let's think about what happens when they achieve world domination. Where do they go from there? What happens when they get what they want? It's most likely still not going to be enough. They will *never* be satisfied because what they truly want, they lost sight of.

Let's turn to the well-known heroes, the villain's counterparts. Again, several come to my mind. What do the heroes want? What kind of background did they come from? What makes them different from the villains?

Love.

Pain.

The heroes still believe they are worthy of love. Surround themselves with the right individuals, even if it's just a few, instead of forcing followers to do their bidding and putting themselves into isolation.

One of my favorite reality shows is *Survivor,* which is more than just a game, it's life. Life constantly challenges you. You either learn how to adapt or you get left behind. Learn how to pass the test or continue to fail, never learning from your mistakes. No risks mean no rewards. You play a safe game; you won't last long. I've watched so many contestants start the game one way and end up doing the opposite of what they wanted to do in order to survive. With your back up against the wall, you will find out what you are capable of. When the morality book gets thrown out, its dog-eat-dog world.

Just with any contest or competition, the end goal is to win. Usually there is a nice prize at the winning circle. A reward. Some cheat in order to get there. Too many are focused on winning that they don't take time to enjoy the journey of growth along the way. Winning is always great. You get bragging rights. Might have something to show for it. But what was sacrificed along the way in order to get there? Can you be proud with every step you took in order to get what you wanted? Sometimes winning isn't always everything. It can be a lonely road. By the time you realize it, it's too late. The same goes for bullying.

What a bully is vying for is love. It's always, love. They're not getting the love they need from a parent, a teacher, a friend, or even a spouse. They use whatever means that gives them the attention that's neglected. Push buttons. Say things they don't mean. The vicious cycle continues year after year. They grasp that their outbursts tend to inflict fear. It rewires their brains. Associate love as pain. When one gives their all and constantly gets nothing in return, it makes one believe they are unlovable. Those scars run deep. Trust in love is broken. Becomes easy to turn to hate. Shields themselves with hate. Gets swallowed whole with unhappiness. Tears other people's happiness apart when really, they are angry at love.

Chapter 5
No

No is a word no one likes to hear. No is a word we hear all the time. Hearing the word gets tiring. No is also a word a bully despises. When you hear the same word so many times, it drives one mad. However, no is necessary in your vocabulary when standing up to a bully. When you tell them no, you are taking their power away. They will throw a fit and go off the rails by whatever means in order to make you cower. Stand tall, even if you're afraid. Don't let them see your fear. They are counting on it. To twist your fear and use it against you when, in reality, their fear outweighs yours. That's right. They are afraid too. In losing their control over you. They don't want you to know that you are stronger than you realize. They are the thunder; you are the lightning. You are more powerful than you think you are and they don't want you to recognize it because once you do, you become a threat. Once they lose their hold, they know they can't get it back, even though they will try repeatedly.

If it becomes physical, report it EVERY time. Don't back down. Don't let others make you feel you are bothering them or making more work for them. It's their job! If they don't like the repeated reports, then that should encourage them to do something about it.

The main objective is, documentation. Concrete proof. Do not make false claims. If you want to be taken seriously, then I repeat, do not make false claims. There's a fable, *The Boy Who Cried Wolf*, and in summary, it's about a boy who cried for help, repeatedly, for attention and then when a wolf actually came around, the villagers didn't come. It's all fun and games until fantasy becomes reality.

When you say nothing and let someone take what they want from you, then they are going to interpret it as being okay. Later on, when you decide to use your voice, they will intimidate in order to silence you to continue getting what they want from you. If you feel uncomfortable around a certain individual, listen to your gut instinct. Use your voice immediately. They will still try to silence you. Tell them no upfront if you feel uncomfortable. If they don't listen, walk away. Do not allow them to hold anything above your head. There is nothing in this world worth being abused into submission. That is what they want, for you to be reliant on them. Do not allow them to get their hooks into you. If they do, it makes things ten times worse for you in the long run.

I'm not an expert in cyberbullying, but it follows the same philosophy. Don't listen to the noise. It's just that, noise. Most bullies are all talk and no action. They feed off of reactions. It makes bullying a whole lot easier. If you don't respond, they have nothing to attack. It's okay to have opinions, but they don't always need to be broadcasted. For every positive thing said, there are always vultures ready to attack. That like to twist your words into something negative. You have nothing to prove to the world. The ones who know you best are the ones that matter. If they are not coming directly to you, the source, they may not be the friends or family you think they are. Bullies like to start stuff for the spite of it. They don't do well in confrontations. They don't know how to handle opposition. They like to corner their prey and toy with it. Give an inch and take a mile. It's all a game to them. Do not play or you will find yourself on that hamster wheel running nowhere.

No means no. However, how you say it makes all the difference. Do not whisper it or form it into a question. The one you say no to will take it as you're not sure and will sweet talk you into saying yes. I mentioned nonverbal cues. This is another example. The bully will pick up on the hesitation in your no. Read your body language that may imply yes. Bullies may not be the sharpest pencils, but they're not as dull either. When it comes to what *they* want, they know what buttons to push. They know what key words to say. They somehow know you're deep, dark secrets because some do their homework.

When dealing with a bully and saying no, make sure that word comes out firm. Never allow them to make you believe they are your only option for whatever lies they feed you. Again, I will state, no means no. Convey it. They will hound you. When they do, respond with silence. The irony, right? However, it's a different kind of silence. What frustrates a bully even more other than the word no? No reaction. Again, nonverbal cues speak volume. When you say no and remain quiet after, walk away. Don't slump. Stand tall. Don't react to the rapid fire that comes from the bully's mouth. They just lost and are throwing a tantrum. If they have something on you, who cares. Don't allow them to hold it over your head. Everyone makes mistakes they regret that shouldn't be publicized, but if it does, you find out who your real friends are and which family members truly have your back. It's a good way to knock out a lot of toxicity in your life. The ones that love you for you are the ones that matter. The rest are all haters and news flash, bullies. Surround yourself with love, not hate. Let them call you all the names in the book. Will it hurt? Absolutely, but only if you give it consent. Drown out the noise with positivity. Do everything that makes you happy. Another thing that irritates a bully. Happiness. At the end of the day, that is what it all comes down to. They don't want to see you happy. They want to rob your happiness because they are miserable. Robbing happiness from others is their currency.

The same is true for manipulators and narcissists. However, they are at an advanced stage over the low totem pole of a bully. A narcissist is at the top. A narcissist won't hold back from acting out in a negative way. Unfortunately, you will have to watch your back. Exactly why it is important to say no right off the bat. The problem will escalate out of control, your control, the longer you yield.

Allow me to give you an example of a narcissist. One I lived with my entire life. One I was supposed to respect because they were my elder. I didn't always respect their actions. When I spoke my mind, I got told quick about it. Who was I to question authority? Especially when I had two authoritative presence above my head. To keep the peace, I backed down with my different viewpoints. First, when I was underage to even question it in the first place and later, many times, I got made out to be the bad guy. I'm not saying every argument of mine was right in the respect of "respecting my elder," but I do recognize now, after writing *The Dark* series, a lot of what I went through was mental abuse. For children, there is a fine line of teaching values and then there is crossing the line in abusing that power when it becomes mental abuse in order to gain what one wants from a child. It's the cruelest thing to put a person in the middle of their child and their mother. Some may not have been intentional to the respect of my elder and some absolutely was intentional. The abuser wants to blame everyone for their problems. They got dished out a hard life and didn't get what they wanted. No million dollars. Nothing on a silver platter. Now, near the end stage of life, they've reverted back to who exactly they always were. A person who is entitled. Let me make something clear, no one, and I mean *no one* is entitled to anything in this life. It's earned every step of the way.

Chapter 6
Standing Up to Bullies

I'm not a licensed expert. It's taken many years of firsthand experience and sitting down to funnel all that I gained into something that might be beneficial to someone one day. I still struggle to stand up to bullies because it's a constant fight not to get dragged under their despair. My first reaction to someone who makes a rude comment or goads is to fire back with the first thing that comes out of my mouth. It's taken years of practice to bite my tongue (not literally) and sometimes I still fail. A person can only take so much bashing before they break their silence, but the better thing to do is disregard the bully.

Disregarding is one of the best things that you can do. The more you disregard your bully's antics, the more they will lose interest. They're not getting a reaction from you. When they don't get what they want from you, they will move on to someone else until they find someone who gives them the reactions they crave. What they also crave is attention and followers. If they get nothing from you, they lose followers. When they lose followers, they find themselves alone. They don't want to be alone. They want to be loved, even if it's the wrong kind of love.

Sometimes disregarding doesn't always work as

they come at you harder. This is where "no" comes in hand. The sooner you put a stop to something that's unwanted, it won't spiral out of control later. If what a bully says or does to you makes you uncomfortable, don't walk away without first telling them what they are doing is unwanted. That is always your first step, using your voice. Make sure when you use it, it's firm. Walk away after. Don't run. Pace yourself as if you are walking down the aisle at a wedding. All eyes are going to be on you, but keep that head held high and embrace the spotlight.

Another thing you can do is use sarcasm. If you are a comedian, this one will be easy for you, but if you're not, it may be difficult. As I mentioned before, use your voice first to convey the behavior is unwanted and then give them the silent treatment. They will goad you in order to get a reaction. It's best to bite your tongue and not respond. Silence is an answer. The words they speak will cut, but don't listen as they bury you with disdain. If you do respond, there are two ways you can do it. With sarcasm or with kindness. Kindness confuses bullies. They get a response, but not the kind that they were going for. They will throw more hurtful words to get you off track, but if you continue to shield the harmful words with kind words, they will eventually lose interest.

Sometimes the best thing to do is avoidance, but don't sacrifice your happiness because a bully hangs out at your favorite place. On the other hand, if you don't need to be at a certain place and the bully is there, go somewhere different. The world is big. The playground is big. Even in your house, there are multiple rooms. If you feel as if a person drains you just by being in the same space as them, find a space where they don't drain you. You are the positive energy. The bully is the negative energy. The bully only sucks that positive energy like a vacuum until you have nothing left. The longer you surround yourself in a negative environment, the more pull that negative has against your positive. Like tug of war. Opposites attract while equivalents deter. Guard your positive. There is too much negative already out there in the world.

Surround yourself with others. If you do find yourself in a place where bullies like to hang out, go with friends. They are your backup. They provide extra strength to that tug of war rope. Have you ever noticed bullies like to surround themselves with followers? Like a pack. Bullies know numbers give them more strength. The same goes for you. They prefer to isolate you for a reason. To lower your self-esteem. If you have friends watching your back, you get a boost in confidence.

If you find yourself boxed in by a bully or bullies, look for your exits. Don't allow a bully to back you into a corner. Avoiding them is always the best, period. Never get into an argument with them because you will lose. Do not allow their followers to surround you. Walk away before they even have a chance to cage you. If you do find yourself confined, don't hesitate to call for help. This is when you want to make your own noise. To attract attention. The kind that will have your bully take flight. If the bully threatens to get physical, don't engage. Stand tall. Resist caving to the whispers of fear. It's what the bully wants. For you to be afraid. Don't show them your fear. When you get an opportunity, walk away with your head held high. It will infuriate them, but most are all talk and no action.

Know who to seek to ask for help. This is hard for me to put in because I usually experience disappointment when reporting bullies. So, this one is geared to children who find themselves bullied. Even then, children are failed too, but it's important to reach out and try instead of dealing with it alone. Children should absolutely be reporting it, but there comes a point in a child's life when they stop because their parents or teachers fail them because bullying is not taken seriously. There is also another reason, adults tend to be afraid of bullies themselves or just don't know how to handle the situation. An act of bullying should be corrected immediately. If the bully is a child, no one should be waiting for another child to report the incident after one has been made. The child bully should be monitored closely and the bad behavior corrected immediately. They will throw a tantrum. As an adult, do not show fear because they will pick up on it and smell it like a hound dog. The adult will then lose complete control of the situation and most likely will never gain it back. With a child bully, there is always a deeper reason for their "bad behavior" in acting out. As an adult dealing with the child bully, you will need to be patient and look for the root problem. It will not come easy since usually by that time the child bully claims up. Don't be another one who gives up and casts them out. They expect that. They don't expect to be challenged. There is something buried in that child bully that even they don't know. What they really need is someone to talk to that will *listen*.

As an adult dealing with a bully, that's not a child,

report the bully as well after you make it clear to the one bullying the behavior is unwanted. Always follow through with actions. Get every incident documented. Keep a record. Bullying is a serious matter. It starts out small and eventually develops into something even more harmful. Manipulating is the next step from bullying until it turns into narcissism. The moment you feel uncomfortable around someone, listen to that inner voice and break ties.

Chapter 7
Bully Behaviors

S ometimes you don't even realize you're being bullied. There's something in the back of your mind that tells you how you're being treated isn't right, but you tend to make excuses. Sometimes you question if you should be questioning certain individuals at all. They are seen in a high respect and have many followers making you outnumbered. Or, someone treats you one way in front of others and another when you're alone with them.

Bullies desire control and dominance. Why does a bully feel the need to control or dominate? Because they live in chaos. They are unhappy. Being able to bring someone down to their level allows them to rise up a notch. It starts in little doses and eventually they lose themselves as it becomes an addiction and they find that it's the only form of control they have in their life.

Bottled up anger. If you read my debut, *The Darkest Side of the Moon*, you may recall I mentioned along the way that anger is used as a shield. Whether you realize it or not, we all use anger as a shield. Why? To avoid being hurt. Our natural response, when threatened, is nine times out of ten, anger. (Yes, I made that statistic up.) You may not agree with me and that's okay. If you are one who easily gets offended, you should dissect that. Truly dissect that to the root cause. (Fun fact, a fortune from my fortune cookie states that "42.7 percent of all statistics are made up on the spot.")

Lacking adequate urge responds. Here is an example. A child running after their ball onto a busy road. How many times have we heard about one ending in tragedy? Ironic, the first *automatic* reaction is usually anger towards the parent(s). It's always easy to put the blame on someone else, but you don't know all the facts. All you know is that a child got hurt running after a ball onto a busy road. You don't know how many times the parent(s) told them to look both ways before crossing a road. In that moment, all the child wanted was their ball, in which the child had a strong urge to run after it. Let's alter the example. Instead of a child, let's reference a dog. How does a dog get trained? Usually treats, but also positive reinforcement, hopefully. Takes a lot of patience and practice. Let's put a squirrel into the mix. The natural, automatic instinct nearly every dog has to a squirrel is to chase it. Even if that dog is taught *not* to chase after the squirrel, the instinct drive is still there. That is something that can *never* be eliminated. The only thing that *can* be done is retraining the brain and even then, the desire still comes naturally. What one wants to happen, when rewiring, is for the dog or child to stop and assess before acting. If no one teaches them, then they will grow to lack adequate urge responds. The same is true for the bully. How is a bully supposed to know how they make one feel when no one taught them or told them?

An absence of empathy. A bully doesn't get what

they want, so they find a different method. They don't want to see someone else happy because they are miserable. Seeing that happiness essentially harms them. Nonverbal cues are taken for granted. How many of you reading this tend to leave subtle hints to others and get upset when they don't receive them the way you hoped? I know I do, all the time. The thing is, no one can read your mind and not everyone is fluent in nonverbal cues. Yes, nonverbal cues are a language. In every language, it's easy to learn and remember the basics. In nonverbal language, a smile is warm and welcoming like "Hello," is in English, or "Hola," in Spanish, "Bonjour," in French, "Hallo," in German, and even "Aloha," in Hawaiian. Have you ever had a negative reaction depending on who might utter the word? How about if it's dripping condescendingly?

Prejudice. We as a society are quick to turn to biases. Quick to misunderstand. We need to break the cycle. Break that mindset. Need to stop thinking inside the box. We are not mindless drones. Need to stop letting others think for us. We are all being treated as robots and every day choices are taken from us without us even realizing it. We lose the ability to do basic things for ourselves, like manually balancing a checkbook. We're not robots, we are complex human beings with emotions that are forced to be suppressed. We were never designed to be automatic. Suppressing our emotions is extremely harmful to our mentality. Depression should not be automatically treated with medication as there are natural ways that should be utilized first. Medication does not fix the root cause of depression as it only numbs it and gives the individual, for the most part, the wrong mindset. Medication is not going to fix being in a hopeless situation that drains one's mentality. Sometimes one has no control. The only control one does have is how they respond to the situation. The same goes for every physical or mental disease/disorder when diagnosed. You can either let yourself sink and drown or fight to stay above the surface. How do I know this? I recently battled depression. A different side of depression that ran deeper to the core than just being down and upset. Unless you walk in someone else's shoes, you have no idea what they are going through. The demons they face. The struggles they overcome. I fought back against depression, without medication. When we suppress our feelings, it's only pressure that boils within that, over time, builds up and eventually explodes like a bottle of soda. Emotions will erupt like lava from a volcano destroying everything in its path. Not everyone has a healthy outlet. Writing is my outlet. By suppressing emotions, you are allowing yourself to live in the dark when we are all meant to live in the light. Dark is hate. Hate is Satan. Light is love. Love is God.

Accountability for their actions. Accepting responsibilities for one's actions is surrendering to vulnerability. We all make mistakes, but we don't always like to admit to them. Admitting to a mistake is admitting that you were wrong. Is viewed as a weakness. Lowers self-esteem. It's like walking out into the middle of an active battlefield to wave a white flag and hoping you survive.

False supremacy. Why does everyone want to win a million dollars, or the lottery, or Publisher's Clearing House? What does winning that money represent? You may have many personal reasons and ideas in what you would do with that money. At the end of the day though, "winning," is the key word. Why does one enter competitions? Why does one enter contests? Why does everyone who is lucky enough to be selected as a contestant on *Survivor* want the title "Sole Survivor"? Does not winning also give you bragging rights?

Blame game. As I mentioned earlier, no one likes to admit to making mistakes or that they were wrong. Bullies have insecurities too. They may be hard to see because they are masters at burying them behind rude and toxic behavior. There is a domino effect that starts earlier on. They had a bad childhood. They had a defect in their biological structure. They had a bad marriage. Basically, they had a lot of bad luck in their lifetime. It's always easy for them to point fingers and blame others for their problems. Subconsciously, though, they take all of that bad and funnel it as being unlovable. All they know is the bad. That people are quick to give up on them. It's easy for one to turn their back then to stay and understand why.

Chapter 8
Mental Bullying

Making rude comments about others is more than just bullying. It's mental abuse. A serious matter. Mental abuse leaves unseen scars that are imprinted and shapes a person into who they become. Eventually, there will come a point where the one being abused has enough and lashes out. Usually it's in a negative way.

It's okay to be different. It's *not* okay to call out every different thing about a person. That's judgement. Leave judgement to a court of law or God. Why does their differences offend you? Don't you fight every day to just be yourself without judgement? That is all everyone in this world wants. To be free to be themselves without the constant harassment for being different. In the end, what is done is rebellion. Every time someone tells a person to be someone they're not, they will find a way to rebel. An extreme haircut. A piercing. A tattoo. Drugs. Alcohol. Unfortunately, some rebellious actions end in tragedy. The more something is threatened to be taken away, the more it's desired. It's only human nature.

Everyone bullies. Even the experts. Doctors, lawyers, politicians, cops, coaches, and even pastors, to name a few. The problem is, most don't realize it.

Their position gives them a higher power and the behavior becomes normalized. They step into that higher power and often times are unable to separate from it. Sometimes they use that power to exploit *their* views as lines become blurred, abusing that power. Some are aware of what they are doing and some aren't.

Cyberbullying. Why do people feel the need to hide behind a computer screen to say spiteful words? Why do people hide behind an electronic device and impersonate a celebrity? They lack self-confidence. It's easier to speak their mind when they know certain repercussions won't follow. Easier to be themselves knowing their face is masked behind a screen. Easy to tear someone else down while lifting their ego. The problem is, it will never fully satisfy their appetite. Like eating air. Zero calories.

Let's take a look at relationships. Often, they are started and continue to build with nothing but lies. Small lies that turn into big lies. If one cannot be honest with themselves first in what they truly want in a relationship, then it's going to fail. No one should *ever* settle for anything less than what they want. It's one of the most difficult things to do, handing someone else the key to your heart. It's vulnerable and raw. If you hand the key to the wrong individual, it can destroy you. Always guard your heart. Don't be quick to hand over the key. If something seems off, listen to your instinct. No matter how much you want to ignore it, I guarantee there are red flags buried that need uncovered. If you give them your all and get nothing in return, that is a huge red flag.

As a society, we are always looking for "the one."

Why? Why is everyone rushing to get married? Rushing to have children? Rushing to rush life away? You can't love someone else if you don't love yourself first. A marriage is more than a partnership. It's a collaboration of two unique individuals. If you are not one who works well on a team, then rushing into a marriage will most likely not succeed. Accept an individual for their differences. Every agreement starts with trust. If one does not go into an agreement with honesty, it won't work in the end. Be honest, always, and work on finding middle ground before committing to something that is supposed to be permanent. If honesty is not received well, then they are not the one.

Before anyone decides to have children, they should ask themselves why they want a child to begin with. A child won't take the loneliness away. A child won't fix a marriage. A child is a lifetime commitment. I see way too many women having children for all the wrong reasons. Eventually, what happens is the child starts to become resented. Children experience the world differently and it's in the parents' actions that reveal underlying emotions. Children can read it loud and clear what is buried within. Their "bad behavior" stems from that. If they feel unloved and unwanted, they spiral down a bad path believing they are unlovable. A toxic mindset.

Why do people do the wrong things? Sometimes one has to make a mistake in order to learn from it. Other times, it's a cry for help. They don't feel seen. They don't feel heard. No one is listening to them. We should not have to pay someone to listen to our problems in order to get the help that's needed from the ones closest to us. When pressure becomes too much and one has a breakdown, it should not be labeled as some diagnosis. That's really providing the wrong mindset. Gives the individual an excuse to blame it on something else instead of understanding what the underlying issue really is. The true underlying issue in most cases is being unhappy. There is something in that individual's life that they are not in control of that causes them to be unhappy whether it's a family issue, a work issue, a friend issue, or a relationship issue. They fear speaking up because the majority of the time they are just silenced.

If you don't understand something, ask! No one should ever make anyone feel inferior in asking for help and be seen as "stupid" for asking. Everyone learns differently. Some can sit through a lecture that lasts for hours and comprehend the material, while others cannot. I'm one of those others. I learn very little in a lecture setting. Other types of learners are visual or hands-on. I'm a bit of both. Some things I can see once and understand while other things I need a hands-on approach. What others take for granted, every day, is that others know what they know. No, they don't. How are you supposed to know something without properly being told or shown? Sometimes it takes several times for a person to be able to properly grasp the information. The key ingredient in everyone's frustration is miscommunication. Some people don't communicate their needs because they are afraid. Some just don't know something others may view as being basic.

Everything you see and hear is some form of mental bullying into changing yourself into becoming someone else. Looks, diets, etc. We are human beings.

Imperfect. If we were all meant to be perfect, we would all be gods. If you want to enhance your appearance with makeup, do it for you, no one else. If you want to drop another waist-size, do it for your health, not because of the latest diet craze. Don't always be quick to follow, you'll just become easy prey. Don't always be quick to listen to the noise, it's just that noise. Listen to your inner voice more than the noise. Drown the negative with positive. Avoid mental hot spots, like social media. There's delete and block options for a reason. Use them before the cycle has a chance to begin. Surround yourself with positive and uplifting individuals.

Chapter 9
Bullying in the Workplace

Why do the good employees leave? Because they are neglected. When you take someone for granted, they will *never* stay. The problem is ALWAYS management. When a person is treated like a machine and not as a human being, what is the point in staying? A job is more than a job. It's a livelihood. That livelihood should give one enjoyment. The quote by Debbi Fields is absolutely true: "You have to have passion when you're finding a recipe for a career. If you love what you are doing, you'll never work a day in your life." When you first wake up in the morning, you should not dread a new day, you should be excited to start a new one. Each new day is a chance to begin again. It should not be mundane. Should not be a repeat of the day prior.

If you are giving your all, but being ignored and getting nothing in return, that is a red flag that you are not being valued as an individual at your place of work. You need to seriously consider moving on. My work ethic is based on the way I'm treated. Praises go a longer way than criticism. If I'm ignored on a daily basis and only mistakes are pointed out, I won't go above and beyond.

Everyone struggles. At the workplace, the greatest

fear is being fired because then there's the unknown of how to earn an income. In reality, if a supervisor is threatening to have your job and you are doing everything in compliance with the workplace codes, that is bullying. If a supervisor or manager is going out of their way targeting you with that firing carrot dangling over your head, that is bullying. They are at a higher power and are using it to their advantage to get what they want from you. Sometimes, it's because they are addicted to the power and other times it's because they are getting pressure from upper management themselves. Let me tell you something, there are PLENTY of open positions. Reevaluate *your* needs and never settle for anything less. I promise, the right job is out there for you with the right group of individuals. If you start a new job and find it doesn't fit with *your* needs, what is stopping you from looking? Yes, the unknown is scary and the grass may not always be greener on the other side, but you'll never find greener grass if you continue to stay where you are not appreciated.

When a person starts a job, the way an individual is trained is everything. If they are not trained properly from the beginning, it will be a hard habit to break when they are taught the "correct way." No one should ever make a new employee feel like they are bothering them when asking questions. When that happens, that causes the new employee to stop asking questions. If they don't understand something, they either stop caring or struggle to figure it out for themselves, which gets frustrating. The job of the trainer is to be patient with the new employee until they understand the material. If a workplace has multiple individuals training an employee, that is cause for concern. Everyone teaches differently. Everyone works differently. Everyone grasps differently. The employees being trained should all be on the same page and they won't be if they all experience a different method to perform a job that has no standard guidelines set in place. There should always be a plan of action *before* the new employee starts their first day. If the time of day is not taken serious for that new employee, chances are they won't last long.

What workplace doesn't have drama? As individuals, we are all unique and have different values, which is okay. What is not okay is excessive drama and gossip. Why do people gossip in the first place? The main reason, they are unhappy. They like to start stuff and prey on the weak. Sound familiar? It should, classic bullying. Of course, it can escalate to manipulation and even narcissism. Let's take a deeper dive at some examples I've experienced over the years, first with a supervisor.

There was an extra training class offered that I was interested in partaking. A continuation of one I had already participated in. As soon as an email was sent out with the dates the training was being offered, I emailed my supervisor immediately, the same day, within minutes. The response I received was that they would check in with the manager. At the time, I thought that was odd, as I had not had the same experience when I asked for approval for the prior training. I didn't make a fuss. I waited to hear back. Meanwhile, other employees weren't shy of talking in the office and others who were interested, that had taken the same prior training class, asked if I was going to be taking the continuous training. I informed I was waiting back from my supervisor, which they thought was odd as they got approved immediately. I let a day slide before reaching back out to my supervisor and was given a lame excuse. I kept watch as the slots were quickly filling and waited a few days for my supervisor to get back to me after "following up" with the manager. When the slots got near single digits, I sent an email straight to the manager expressing my interest and hoping they would give my supervisor approval to approve me for the training. The response back was not what I was expecting. That it was up to the supervisor to give approval or not. It was clear to me that the supervisor did not need the manager's approval. Soon after my supervisor pulled me aside to a private room and started spouting off about guides that I had made and shared with the office among some other things. In the end, I was approved for the continuous training, but my relationship with my supervisor was never the same. They were not happy that I went over their head and caught them in a lie. I'm certain if I had not sent an email to the manager, I would have missed the training opportunity. For whatever reason, that supervisor had an issue with me before the whole situation even took place and abused their power. I felt the negative vibe. Brought it out into the light and they overreacted because I stood my ground. I was not an employee they were used to that fought back respectfully.

Let's move onto another example of office drama. This time with some coworkers. I'll try my best to make a long story short. I started with a big group of new hires. Bonded with an older lady. It was the two of us in the beginning and then it turned into three. We would take breaks together and walk discussing the office politics of course. The older lady and I had a falling out. A misunderstanding. I was just trying to be helpful, but believe she was embarrassed by it and basically overreacted. I gave her some space, like she asked. A few days turned into a few weeks that turned into months. One day I happened to stumble upon her in the bathroom and asked, "Why do you hate me?" That's the negative vibe I got. We were so close and then it was so cold around her. She claimed she didn't hate me. We ended up hugging it out and "making up." However, the hug still felt cold. I kept my distance. Meanwhile, I was keeping quiet about the whole situation to the other girl, trying to keep her from getting caught in the middle of it. Out of the blue one morning walking into work, she grilled me about calling her "sensitive." I was flabbergasted. Wondered where she heard that as I had never said that out loud. Then it hit me. I had let it slip when I was "making up" with the older lady in the bathroom, who even agreed to that assessment. It was clear to me then that she was not over her issue with me and that I was the one who had ended up in the middle of them. News flash, if you are offended by an honest comment about being sensitive and throwing a fit about it, you my dear are sensitive.

Let me tell you something that I've learned over the years. The customers are NOT always right. We, as a society, need to stop catering to rude customer's needs and allowing them to bully and harass employees. Customers are *not* the ones that make a company shine. Employees are. Without employees, there would be no business, period. If employees are leaving left and right, that is a red flag that there is a problem. It should never be swept under a rug. Taking anonymous surveys does little to narrow down the true problem. It usually has something to do with management and most employees are too afraid to speak honestly for fear of being targeted and/or fired. A promise that there will be no retaliation means nothing. How many times have we heard on the news or seen a movie or TV show that someone who had a restraining order met a tragic end? Makes great entertainment, but it also installs fear. There are so many campaigns out there rallying to ask for help, yet when you do, you don't usually get the help you need. Trust me, I've experienced it firsthand. I understand why people feel the need to take matters into their own hands. Desperation. And yet, we all still wonder why people act out with "extreme behavior." When one reaches the end of their rope, there is no place for one to go other than rock bottom. It always circles back to listening. Truly listening. Stopping what you are doing and giving someone your complete attention. There are *always* subtle signs. Management needs to work on paying attention and listening with an open mind without easily getting offended.

Chapter 10
The Manipulator

As you might have taken notice, I view bullying to having different levels. The lowest is bullying itself. The next is manipulating. That "bad behavior" from childhood only escalates when not corrected immediately. The more someone gets away with something, the more confidence they gain that they are entitled to receive attention the wrong way. Empathy goes out the door as they become a puppet master in toying with emotions.

There's another term you might have heard. Gaslighting. Manipulators like to pour fuel, disdainful words, onto the fire, your emotions. Prey on self-doubt and twist you in all different kinds of directions until you lose sight of reality. The more you hear negative contempt, the more you start to believe it. Imagine hearing the word "can't" on repeat, daily. The more you hear that you can't do something, your mind will automatically go to that place and you'll eventually stop even trying. In reality, the manipulator is redirecting their insecurities onto you. They don't want to see you be successful and try. They are bringing you down to their level of thinking. Let me make it clear, you can achieve anything you put your mind to. Sometimes failure is there to knock you down, but the only one keeping you down is yourself. Everything is achievable in a worthy fight as long as you have the courage to keep fighting and never back down, even if you stand alone. Let me tell you something, the road less travelled is nice and quiet with plenty of oxygen to breathe and sunshine to bathe in. Energizing.

Most manipulators don't realize what they are doing is wrong. They might have started out with the realization, but when no one called them out on it the behavior became normal. It's all about their needs and wants. They want something, the only thing they know is how to get it by force. They didn't get something in life, so they don't want to see you succeed at it. They swim in a pool of bitterness and self-loathe.

Let's redirect our attention to some examples. The best ones that come to mind are with parents and my observations in real life and in the movies. Most times, a movie is more than a movie. If you pay attention, there is always something that movie is trying to teach you. The ones you connect with are the ones you understand because you live it. The ones you don't fully connect with are the ones you should pay more attention to.

Every day there are parents pushing expectations and pressures onto their children. They didn't achieve their dream and want what they think is best for their children. Two ways kids respond. Either they push too hard not to disappoint their parent(s) or try to convey it's not what *they* want, but their parents don't listen. Either way, it will never make the child happy because it's not what the child wants. It's a dream someone else wants for them. A very good example of this is sports. Who are the ones most likely to go off on the referee?

Parents. Coaches are the second. Usually due to pressure from parents. At a young age, whatever sport a child gets interested in, should stay that way. It should not be the parent's dream to see their child achieve a dream they never could. When it turns from what the child wants into what the parent wants for their child, that child is going to lose interest.

Let's move onto coaches. In the beginning, it's for the love of the game. Soon, it turns south real fast. They start doing whatever it takes to get a win even if it resorts to manipulating. Playing a game is not always about winning. It's about achieving growth. Sometimes you have to lose in order to win.

The last is politics. Sport politics. I used to play basketball. I loved playing basketball. There is still a place in my heart for it, but when I was in school the love of the sport fizzled out. All I wanted to do was play the game to the best of my ability. During practice one night, I pushed myself too far and ended up breaking my wrist all for the sake of winning bragging rights for my team. During games, I wasn't the star player and hardly got the ball. When I did, I made a shocking shot that the crowd yelled should have been a three-pointer. For a young girl in elementary school, yeah it should have been a three-pointer. When I moved on from elementary school, I went to try-outs, but the one crucial thing was missing. The love of the sport itself. To the school you had to be in tip-top shape and it was all about winning. I lost interest and quit. A disheartening decision, but I still love the sport and shoot hoops for the fun of it.

Chapter 11
The Narcissist

When visualizing tiers of bullying, I consider narcissism to be at the top. The vilest place a bully can go. Extremely difficult to get them off their high horse of self-interest. By the time a bully reaches this level, they are too far gone. Delusional even. Will go to extreme lengths to get what they want from you. Questioning them is a sin as they've put themselves up so high on that pedestal, out of reach, that their heads are in the clouds. Become numb to feeling anything. See nothing wrong with their actions. Go to whatever lengths to make you cower to them. Believe they should be admired as some kind of hero when in reality they are just the villain allowing their inner demons take control. Too far down the wrong path blinds reason.

They do not like to be challenged or held accountable for their actions. Will spin it around to make it look as if you are the bad guy. Act a certain way in public, but behind closed doors their true colors come out. Will resort to violence in order to get what they want. Toy with your emotions feeding you your own insecurities to gain power over you.

A narcissist will prey on the thing you fear the most and use that as their leverage to keep you in line. Turn everything around on you. Plant self-doubt. They don't want you to think for yourself. They don't want you to question them. They play the victim very well. There is no reasoning with them. They have in their mind they are right and everything you do is wrong. Are quick to criticize, but refuse to lift a finger. You are nothing but their slave. Will never measure up to their expectations. Are expendable if uncooperative. It's the darkest side of bullying.

There's a reason one feels energy draining when they are around certain individuals. That is your inner warning sign to leave and never look back. Its true opposites attract. The negative energy a narcissist expels will suck away your positive energy like a black hole until nothing is left. When it's gone, it's a long, hard process to rebuild. Those unseen scars will always remain. A constant reminder. If you want to funnel it into a word that you can associate with, it's trauma.

Not everyone has the luxury to leave though. You might be one who finds themselves trapped in a situation outside of your control. There is only so much you can do. The key is, do the things that make *you* happy. Find an outlet. Writing, music, walking, or reading. Immerse yourself in it. Soak up the sunshine. Try new things, even if it's alone. Never believe their lies. Everyone has a choice. Live a miserable life blaming the world for their problems or living life to the fullest embracing and enjoying the smallest of things. I've said it once before and I'll say it again, money doesn't buy happiness, only a dose. When one gains material things, it never fulfils their happiness for long. Everything is replaceable. Everything has an expiration date. The ones who are unhappy believe in a false lie that they can buy their happiness. One can buy the biggest house, the most expensive car, dozens of shoes, or whatever it is that speaks money, but at the end of the day, when everyone leaves, chances are they are still going to feel alone. Loneliness takes you to dark places. Tampers with your mind. No drugs or alcohol is going to take the loneliness away. They only bring more demons.

A narcissist is so far down that dark pit that happiness brings them pain. Like stepping out into the sunshine from a dark room. It's going to sting your eyes. Enough to make you retreat. It takes time to adjust. Adjust is necessary. The longer one lives in bitterness and resentment lines are blurred and hope is lost.

Boundaries are vital when dealing with a narcissist. Their mouth is their weapon as they throw harmful words like daggers. Do not let them goad you into a shouting match. You will lose. Let the venomous words pour out. Never believe them. Speak calmly for yourself, but do not get caught up on that hamster wheel that spins you nowhere. Remember, they are the thunder, you are the lightning. You have the power to either let them bring you down, or rise above.

If you are dealing with a narcissist who is physical, the best advice I can give is, don't be an easy target. In no way am I an expert in that department though. Never be ashamed to ask for help. Surround yourself with support. Avoid putting yourself in a position where you are alone with them. If you do find yourself alone with them, don't talk back. It only further engages their rage. No one should live in fear.

Chapter 12
Bias

Bias.

Something we are *all* guilty of. It's in our nature as we are human. Sinful creatures ever since that bite was taken from the forbidden fruit. One can act as perfect as can be and above it all, but at the end of the day no one is perfect. We all have faults. We all have flaws. If we were all perfect, we would have achieved world peace by now.

I am guilty of bias as well. I try hard to fight against it, but it's just in my human nature. I've learned differently, experienced things differently, overcome things others have not. What sets me apart from many others is I'm not quick to verbalize it. Social media makes it too easy to voice your opinions, and there is nothing wrong with having an opinion, but once you publish those opinions, you can't take them back. You can retract a statement all you want, it doesn't matter. The harm was already done.

I went to a local playground with a good friend of mine and her children, four and one. The first time I got to meet them since COVID-19 took over the world. My friend's daughter is a little tomboy and she ran off with two young boys a little older than her. They seemed a mix of annoyed and accepting as they took turns climbing and sliding.

My first thought about the two boys were that they appeared the classic bully type. While they were doing their thing, they were watching with an eagerness as my friend's son was having fun with a spiky ball gifted to him. Another little girl wanted in on the fun. Since there were two spiky balls and the other wasn't being utilized, I made the little girl's day allowing her to get some play time. Kids are usually focused on one thing, wanting what they can't have. They don't understand the rules and they don't care. All they see is someone else having fun and wanting to join in. Kids have no boundaries. When they are forced to go against their nature, they cry. They just want to be included. Sound familiar? It should. That is basically what we all want. To be included. To not feel alone.

The two older boys were having fun while their, I presume, father watched from a bench. They were not being unruly, but they were sliding headfirst down the slide and rushing up to the top past the other little girl. Kids don't understand their carefreeness can potentially have consequences. It is up to the parent(s) to guide them. Direct them to the right frame of mind. That carefreeness eventually looks to be unruly to others.

I do not have human children of my own, but I have a strong maternal instinct. My friend's daughter and son I treated as my own. I kept my attention on the older boys. Although they did a few things I wasn't fond of, it wasn't my place to say anything, since they were not doing harm to the other children on the playground. I noticed how they kept eyeing the balls. Gave me some looks as well, but they seemed uncertain about me as I was uncertain about them. I believe they picked up on my vibe that I was watching them like a hawk.

At one point, while I was assisting my friend's daughter as she was climbing up to the highest slide, the one boy opened up and told me about a grasshopper on the back of the lower slide. It wasn't a real grasshopper. It was a molded one underneath the slide. Had no idea it was there.

I can't recall how it exactly played out after. All I know is one of the balls was offered to one of the boys and they lit up with happiness. Boys are boys and they did play rough and enjoyed kicking the ball around, but the most shocking and amazing thing happened as well. The older of the two rolled the ball gently to my friend's one-year-old son, at his level, to keep him included. It was the two boys, my friend's son, and me tossing the ball back and forth. Something so simple and yet made all the difference. I was able to relax and they were able to relax as well once we were all on the same page.

I was wrong to judge them right out of the gate. I'm not afraid to admit it. Admitting you are wrong is the hardest thing for everyone to do. There is absolutely nothing wrong in making mistakes. Mistakes are how you learn and grow. If you never acknowledge your mistakes, you never learn or grow. Acknowledging is always the first step in adapting a better you.

Now, do I believe those two boys might grow into becoming bullies? Absolutely. You want to know why, because there are not enough people out there who will show them kindness and want to include them. Maybe they won't become the classic bullies you find at school. Maybe my act of kindness made a difference in their lives. I don't know if it will be enough, but I can only hope. That's the bias talking in me. See, still guilty. All I know is, I've seen enough in my lifetime to predict. When one is constantly surrounded by negativity, it rubs off on a person or child. It's hard to stay positive when the toxins of negativity drain you on a constant basis. Infects you until you become bitter and resentful. Hatred is like a weed. The more you try to eliminate it from your garden, the more it sprouts. You either learn to appreciate it for what it is and represents or you continue to go to war with it until you've destroyed the ground with cancerous chemicals that end up being harmful to your well-being. At the end of the day, that weed represents life. It's fighting to live. Has purpose. Isn't that what we are all fighting for? To be understood and accepted for who we are as we are and not having to change for no one?

Chapter 13
Ignore

Raise your hand if you like to be ignored. Let's rephrase the question. Raise your hand if you like to be ignored for the rest of your life. If you raised your hand, and not in a mocking way, you need to evaluate why. Human beings are social by nature. No one likes to be ignored, no one. Why do you think social media is so popular? It's a way to express oneself and get attention. Has the power to connect you with like-mind individuals that you find are not close to home.

Why do we fear meeting someone new in person? We fear being ourselves will rub them the wrong way. Why do we dress to impress? We want to put our best selves forth. Why do we pretend to be someone we're not? We fear being alone.

Being ignored is the worst feeling ever. I detest it. Whether intentional by others or not, being ignored has a negative impact on your mentality. You don't know what to think. Are you being ignored because you did something wrong? Did something to offend someone? Are you just not as well liked by others? If you can't get a simple hello, are you just a forgotten memory?

Everyone has busy lives, I get it, I do. I have a busy life too, but I also take time to smile and say a warm hello when I pass strangers when out walking or out in about. I might not have time to talk for hours on end, but sometimes five minutes makes a big difference. You never know who you cross paths with and what they are struggling with. You could end up saving a life without even realizing it. That one positive experience can make all the difference in someone who may be drowning in a negative mindset. May be the drive they need to make it another day.

Labels are being applied to normal human emotions that are being misunderstood as "bad behavior" in society. Labels are also quickly applied as an excuse for that "bad behavior" and treated with medication. Mediation is not always the solution. A lot of times it's only a Band-Aid. It won't stick forever. Ignoring the root cause of a problem is never a solution. It will be frustrating to get to, but ignoring it altogether will only cause more problems in the long run.

Let's apply ignoring to bullying. Remember, one of the ways to stop the unwanted behavior was to give them the silent treatment? Well, yeah, that is ignoring. That's what you sometimes need to do, but remember, a bully is a human being too. They have feelings. They want attention, but they are trying to get it the wrong way. You can avoid them to prevent the triggering response, but if you find yourself in the same vicinity as your bully, say hello. Smile even. You won't get results right away, trust me, but if you direct some positivity their way, it might change how they treat you. Not always, but you will never know unless you try. What do you have to lose? You want to reinforce good behavior. Acknowledge them with positive manners. What might happen in the long run is them losing interest in you, but maybe, just maybe, they might acknowledge you too in a positive way.

What is worse than a scorned individual? One who is ignored. They fester in loath. Are unable to express themselves. Have no one to talk to that will listen. Ignoring is a two-way street. Sometimes it's good, sometimes it's bad. It takes a great deal of practice to comprehend when it's best to apply it. Observation is key. Pay attention to nonverbal cues. Again, nonverbal cues are a different language and very easy to misread. What applies to one individual doesn't always necessarily apply to another. What one individual is comfortable with doesn't automatically mean every individual is comfortable with. Making fun of that individual for your ignorance makes a fool out of you.

Let's redirect our attention to technology and social media. One of the best inventions and worst inventions made. Makes ignoring easier and bullying easier. Someone you are not fond of sent a message, ignore. Lines are blurred between not interested and games being played to keep one on the hook. Toying with emotions. It's *never* okay to use someone's emotions against them. If you are not interested, put on the big pants and tell them. If they can't handle no, it's their problem, not yours, but when you start ignoring them, it's not going to blindside them.

Social media. Started out as something good and went south real fast. At the end of the day, most of your "friends" or "followers" are strangers. Let's reverse back to our childhood where hopefully you were told "stranger danger." You *must* treat those "friends" or "followers" as potentially dangerous. Do not allow yourself to be easy prey. Always keep your guard way up. It's easy to lie to someone you don't know to make yourself appear more. Hard to see or read true intent. If the conversation is one sided, there is a reason for that. They are gathering as much intel from you to feed you exactly what you want to hear. Don't be quick to give them what they want and don't get trapped in an endless cycle. Turn off the temptation so you're not quick to respond. It may be rude to ignore, but in this case, it's necessary. Think before you respond. Again, you can't take something back once it's published. Silence is answer enough.

Ignoring in the workplace. Can't always be done as certain tasks require teamwork while other jobs require customer service. You can't ignore a rude customer. It's your job to service them, but not to be harassed. The boss may not always have your back in the matter, depending on the boss's people's skills. Your poor attitude will only add fuel to the fire. Sometimes it's best to give the customer what they want, even if the mistake was theirs, but when they disrespect you with foul language or harsh unnecessary words, that's when you stand your ground and ask for reinforcements. Again, your boss may not always have your back. It's perfectly acceptable to be upset about it because they failed you. Be honest and convey it in a professional way. You still have to maintain a professional affiliation with your boss while at work, but if it's not business related, then that is where it ends. The key word, *business*. That stands with co-workers too. If the job requires you working together to achieve a goal for the business, it's business first. Afterwards, anything personal gets ignored. If they respect you as an individual then they will want to address the problem. If not, you're better off without them in your life.

Chapter 14
Kindness

W hy are we afraid to be kind? Because we don't want to be taken advantage of. No one wants to put their heart and soul on the line, only to be crushed beyond the hope of repair. The thing is, kindness also revives. Removes the toxins of negativity and replaces it with an energizing antidote of positivity. Kindness should *never* be something we are afraid of. We *need* kindness to chase away the dark. Kindness is sunshine. Necessary after a gloomy day of rain. Necessary after the darkest of nights. Every ray should be bathed in.

A bully's exterior is a frosty tundra. The only way to break through their ice is with warm words. It's going to take a lot of warm words. Changes don't happen overnight. Their unseen scars run deep to their core. Most don't even know how to comprehend their true feelings for they have been suppressed for too long. Are unable to trust that you have their best interest at heart. It's easier to redirect hurt onto others than to recognize the hurt in themselves.

Too many forget the true meaning of an act of kindness. An act of kindness is doing something and expecting *nothing* in return. If you are expecting something in return for being "nice" that is manipulating.

The only currency you should ever expect in return from an act of kindness is a smile and maybe a thank you.

Kindness also provides relief. Don't we all want relief from negativity? Relief from hatred? Relief from misery? So does the bully, even if they don't realize it. When one goes so far down a rabbit hole, it's hard to climb back out. A helping hand is what they need. When one gets so used to pushing away from help, it's hard to trust in help in itself. Asking for help is opening yourself to vulnerability. The last thing a bully wants, is to appear weak. When one asks for help and it's not received well, they close up. Slam the door, lock it, and throw away the key never to be seen again. They reached out and were not given the support they required at the time. It mainly starts in childhood, builds into adolescence, and molds into adulthood.

A tragedy should not strike in order for everyone to set aside their differences and come together to assist. A holiday should not alter one's way of thinking on the days that holidays are not. Even then, most forget the true meaning of the holiday. Too consumed in what they should be doing verses the meaning of the act itself. Again, we are not robots. Take time to dissect what each holiday means to you.

I have been treated with a lot of contempt in my life. Even though I had every right to turn my back on the one who treated me so poorly, I refused to give in. That's what they wanted. That's what they expected. What they didn't expect was for me to push back. To stand up for myself. To stand up for what was right. It was a long hard battle, but in the end, love won along with playing P!nk's song on repeat, "Just Say I'm Sorry." They surrendered to their insecurities and self-loath and let love back in. In doing so, they found peace. Death is merciful. It's not to be afraid of. Why do we truly fear death? Because we fear the unknown. We all just want to be happy. Everything in life is a test. A stepping stone in your journey in order to move towards the right path. Death is not to be afraid of. It's a part of the life cycle. We fear it because we fear that we won't reach a better place. In reality, we are already living in Hell. One of our own creation. It's never too late to change. I am living proof that one can take a negative and turn it into a positive. That you can stay true to your authentic self and be enough as is.

So, how does one truly stand up to bullying? Acts of kindness. All a bully really wants in the end is to be seen, to be heard, to be appreciated, respected for their differences, to have a helping hand, and to be loved. It starts with *all* of us. It's not something to be done 1 day of the year, it's something to be done 365 days.

Kindness starts with being kind to yourself. Kindness is love. You can't love anyone else if you don't love yourself first. Get in the practice of showering yourself with kind words and compliments until it becomes routine and eventually you start believing it instead of the lies. Society has bred our minds to be quick to go into negative thoughts. Break the chains. Retrain your mind. Stand up to bullying once and for all.

Stand Up to Bullying
by M. C. Ryder
(Written April, 17, 2023)

Kicked and pushed around
Feeling at an all-time low
Allowing the whispers of fear
To overrun your mind

Boxed into a corner
Overshadowed by isolation
Overwhelmed in loneliness
Constantly misunderstood

Pre-chorus:
Waiting on a hero
Only one will never come
You have to be your own hero

Chorus:
Break the cycle
Stand tall and firm
Say no
Bullying is abuse
They are the thunder
You are the lightning
Strike them down with your voice

Easy to run your mouth
From the protection of a screen
Easy to feed your ego
By tearing someone down

Pain only becomes an addiction
While stealing other's happiness
Because you lack your own
You'll never find it by knocking others down

Pre-chorus:
Waiting on a hero
Only one will never come
You have to be your own hero

Chorus:
Break the cycle
Stand tall and firm
Say no
Bullying is abuse
You are the thunder
They are the lightning
You know they have the power
To strike you down with their voice

Bridge:
Power
It's all about power
A disguise
When in reality
It's love
Yes, love
That's wanted

Chorus:
Break the cycle
Stand tall and firm
Say no
Bullying is abuse
That only gets struck down
With your voice

We all just want to be loved
Appreciated and valued
For who we are
And to be one with happiness
But it starts with all of us
To stand up to bullying

About the Author

Award-winning author of *The Dark* series, M. C. Ryder has been composing stories, poems, and lyrics from the beginning of time when reading became a hobby. The sky is the limit, but enjoys exploring the beaten path both figuratively and literally. Resides in the Keystone State with a clowder of felines who rule the house. Enjoys long trail walks during the cozy tinge of Autumn, appreciates music with deep lyrical meaning, and relishes in reading a variety of genres.

Website: https://www.mcryderauthor.com

M. C. Ryder (page)

MCRyder0

mcryder0

CPSIA information can be obtained
at www.ICGtesting.com
Printed in the USA
BVHW040824090723
666955BV00005B/121